TANA HOBAN

Spirals, Curves, Fanshapes & Lines

Greenwillow Books, New York

The full-color photographs were reproduced
from 35-mm slides.
The typeface is Benguiat Gothic.

Printed in Singapore by Tien Wah Press
First Edition   10 9 8 7 6 5 4 3 2 1

Library of Congress Cataloging-in-Publication Data
Hoban, Tana.
Spirals, curves, fanshapes and lines / by Tana Hoban.
p.   cm.
Summary: Introduces the concepts of spirals, curves,
fanshapes, and lines through photographs of bananas,
a broom, birds, and other objects and things.
ISBN 0-688-11228-5 (trade).
ISBN 0-688-11229-3 (lib. bdg.)
1. Geometry—Juvenile literature.   [1. Shape.]
I. Title.   QA445.5.H63   1992
516'.15—dc20   91-30159   CIP   AC

This one is for my sister, Freeda

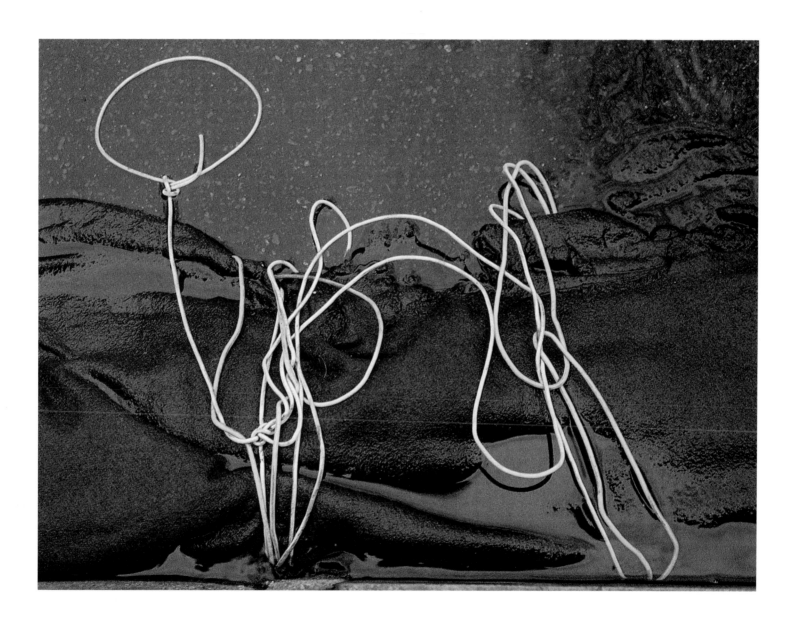